*Enjoy!*

*Carol Boland*

# The Overture

## A collection of poems

## Carol Boland

Boland Press

First published in 2012
Copyright @ Carol Boland
All rights reserved. No part of this
publication may be reproduced or
transmitted by any means electronic,
mechanical, photocopying or otherwise,
without the prior permission of the publisher
Boland Press
Grove Mill
Hollyfort
Co. Wexford
http://bolandpress.blogspot.com

A CIP catalogue record for this book
is available from the British Library
ISBN 978-1-907855-04-7
Cover design by Boland Press

Printed in Ireland by Conway Media Ltd

For the Sheds

Acknowledgement is given to the following
publications where poems, or versions of
them, have appeared:
Bray Arts Journal (various issues)
The Scaldy Detail, (Scalltamedia, 2010)
The Poetry Bus, Issue 1
Strands of Silk, (Boland Press, 2010)
Anniversary, Wicklow Writers Anthology,
(Boland Press, 2010)
*Fanning the flame* broadcast on Lyric FM 2010
Tidings (C. Boland, 2008)
Razzamatazz and Other Poems,
(Leaf Books, 2006)

**Carol Boland** was born in Dublin in 1954. She has lived in Dublin, London and Wicklow Town, and now resides in a small village in County Wexford.

A performance poet, workshop facilitator and novelist, Carol is also editor of *The Space Inside* arts magazine.

*The Overture* is her first collection of poetry.

# Contents

## The Overture

**Notes**

**The Overture**

# Aphrodisia

Like Cleopatra she enters the room
in full sail, purple silks of her royal barge
billowing in the scented air.

A thing of beauty by ancient standards
she glides like a painted Aphrodite
a soporific blend of cassis and cinnamon.

Diamond droplets sway from her lobes
move to jangle of beaten silver bangles
tingling a sea of faces, sending a finger
to the bridge of his slipping spectacles.

And as her bow cuts deep into Tarsus
another Anthony stands in its wake
intoxicated by the jasmine dipped sails
and shaky on his newly-wed sea-legs
he steadies himself against the creaking rail.

## Lost in Laurence's Arabia

I ride out of the desert
      looking to conquer Aqaba
clothes stiff with fear
      eyes green with lust

carrying hope in my left
      despair in my right as
cannons stand firm
      gaze open-mouthed to sea.

And I find victory in the desert's dust
      but no golden librettos
only a chest lined with paper
      and a promise to pay the bearer.

## The Overture

Play me something
says the fisherman
as he lays her hands on the keys
takes his seat in the front row.

She takes her time
removes a layer of dust
from the piano's skin
for this is her baby
her grand Russian spruce
grain long and close
crafted to stroke a clear tone.

She feels his eyes in the high
gloss of ebony sail,
offers him her time
arranging his fingers -
schooled for tying knots
not netting melodies,

and hand over hand
they practice the bowline
reef knot
the tying
untying.

## Eyes closed

Dreaming fingers dip me
in candle wax and tiffany
carry me over sliced ivory
like a blue dragon flying
in deep-space memory

until I disappear
in strains of mahogany
measured tones of ebony
ounce by short ounce
shimmying ever closer
to the end of love

where a trip
a stumble
stalls the two-step
causes time to side-step
lose rhythm.

## Fanning the flame

I twirl him
in a butterfly net
as he circles my hair
on multi-coloured
wings of possibilities
until the strain
of the last game
snaps me
like a string
of worry beads
scatters my
alternatives
bouncing them
high and low on
a stone cold floor.
The only time
he visits now
is on rumours
of his wildness.

## Bassoon players

I might as well
sit howling at the moon
as thread the laces
of a Sunday afternoon
to hold the lift and fall
the deepest croon
of my ensemble
thin and full of grace.

Their days run long
while mine are hewn
from wind-worn sticks
that leave a silent trace
across the hours that
stretch, bend and meld
into the ether of this space.

If offspring are the
timbre in my tune
that halts the rivulets
across my face
can I replace the concert
players' tune and sing
the status quo
back into place?

I might as well
sit howling at the moon
as thread the laces
of a Sunday afternoon.

# Reflections

The scarf
made from Indian gold
lies cautiously on stitches
of an aran knit.

Ears almost hidden
eyes almost black
a pindot beam lights
up a nose that
sniffs away pearls of wax.

And on her face
a mole blinks
and she is blinded
by the purple bruises
under her skin.

A mirror hangs


on a bathroom wall
steam veiling
a mercurial face
in the gloom

only her inner light
shines through
like sparks from
an angle-grinder.

## The Oscars

She wore him
        like an off-the-shoulder dress
black silk prowling
        her painted bones

while he draped her with angles
        tight and obtuse,
dark glassed
        against the glare.

In perfect symmetry
        they scuffed the edges
of a red carpet
        stretched lips and teeth

        inch by red inch.

# Dinner party

An odd number
she sits
and as they whisper
she twists
extract of bark and leaf
to heal their bruises.

Sometimes
in her divine hand
a wand twitches
and for that second
she is worshipped.

In danker days
they would
have burned her
in hazel woods.

I plant a yew


older than Methuselah
wiser than a druid's staff

a leaf
        flat and lanceolate
        greener than the greenest

one seed
        in a scarlet poisoned cup

a bough
        the archer's bow
        durable as the spear found
        lodged in the ribs of a
        straight-tusked elephant.


I heal your roots into the clay
dislodge you from my rib.

# Crossing the bog of Alan

The road undulates
in a timeline of pits and pots
rising and slipping
like an unseen storm.

Seasick
in our ship of fools
we sail on
flatten the earth
brown and bursting
with bodies
spliced with decay.

Who was this ancient man
this giant dandy of beaten bronze
whose manicurist knew him well.

Had he dishonoured the king's wife
pulling her under his blanket
with hands as soft as bog cotton
feeding her buttermilk and cereal.

And when they stabbed him
threaded his arms with twisted hazel
sliced his nipples
did he remember her smell.

## Ladies in Lavender

They grow
straight from the wood
ears like purple corn
bodies long and narrow
stick-like in no-nonsense
brogues that flourish
best in dry soil.

Old-fashioned
in their way
and reminiscent
of lace-fringed
handkerchiefs
peeking from
lavender sleeves,
they once shadowed
fresher gravel
keener verges.

Now this young man
flits between rows
of scented oils
encroaches on
their footpaths
unfulfilled yearnings
turning hardened
hearts to honey

a bee among layers
of fragrant apparel
frightening in his
stinging beauty.

Let the ladies
enjoy this moment
of breathless humidity
before he plucks
his strings for
a grander audience
leaving them to doze
in heat of the day
as comfortable as cats
on a down quilt.

## Stretching out

Rushes sketched
in bog-standard
textbook
leave me lifeless

for in my youth
I stalked
the Real McCoy
stepped from clump
to shallow clump in
bog-holes dipped
in cotton socks

and stretched
an anxious hand
across the turf-
soaked hush
to stroke the
furry hide of a
bull-headed rush.

## The dreaming time

Time waltzes on
                    smaltz
keys to a heart
jingle-jangle
                    tangle


knock-knock
tick-tock


give us a song Bruce
                    forgotten
a line of dreams
                    gone

Tick
          the body's clock
Tock.

# The Jazz Dancer

Swirled in turbulent dust
the fallout unsettles my feet

      in pink ballet shoes
      I was asked to leave -
      too giddy
      I was seven.

Standing by the
smudged winter pane
I watch refuse collectors
shuffle box to box
through chaines
of avenue and road
side-stepping Christmas
windows each one
louder than the past

and I see my future
through pink windolene
as I tap-dance alone
to Nina Simone.

A touch of jazz


Teach me
the twelve bar blues
a touch of jazz
that old pizzazz

so I can swim
in purple pinks
when shadows
lie on garden clatter
mobile chatter
freezing up the sky

and I'll roll out
my old joanna
swing thro'
sun-dried days.

## Still dancing

Are you still dancing in the dark
in stocking feet
humming Cohen
in a hallelujah key
that never opened doors
nor cell of your confinement.

Are you still dancing in the dark
or on a hospital trolley
holes in your socks
skin unevenly stitched
having forced your will
on an unwary Citroen.

Are you still dancing in the dark
in two bare feet
paying no heed
without watch or breath
in the stillness
of the undergrowth.

# The painter and the poet

The house stretches its grey skin
prepares itself for the painter's hand
a slow rhythmic brush into wild cotton
a rebirth of sorts.

A true artist, he strips to the waist
lays down a white sheet on olive ground
paints a shadow on fresh canvas
a rendering of sorts.

A day's artistry on his shoulders
brings sun strokes in need of reparation
so he plucks a leaf from succulent Aloe Vera
grown on the window sill for such a moment

and splits the soft green flesh
with his tender nail, offers
the healing lotion to his healer.

With firm strokes she presses
the open leaf to his skin,
flesh on flesh
skin on skin
a renewal of sorts.

Now, do something for me, she says
handing him a sharp scissors
her finger with a broken nail.

## Reading Akhmatova

Do not judge me
as I read poems
in a Moscow café
for this is my
breathing space –

old men do not stir me
and young ones
I shun for
propriety's sake.

Is that woman behind
me with her lover?
Skin crumples lines
between cup and lip
in silent imaginings as

I sit within a poet's world
keeping seclusion at bay
safe from the torture
of nothing more to say.

And for this I thank you

I swam out of
my depth today
for the first time
in a very long time
warmed bitter
stony waters with
flights of fantasy

imagined
what it would feel like
to permit the lake
take my breath
abandon my skin
to the swim and

like the lady of the lake
ascend with arm
outstretched
excalibur restored.

You remind me

# Memories in a mattress

I wrestle the writhing beast
through the door
heave and pull
at dip and lip
until sullen and withdrawn
winded on its back
it submits in the back garden.

I stand at the foot
of this double-sided slice of my life
so, it has come to this -
twenty years of seeping
blood, milk and tears.

I press the unseen knife to its belly
where each blemish is an act of love,
or a tainted stain
like a birthmark on a pelt
a storyboard
a hide for acts of treason.

Murder on my mind,
I stab the sagging skin
rip open its lumpy recess
spill its guts
discolour the soil
black and white.

And up to my elbow in pleasure
I feel it squeal under my hand
as I reach for its backbone
dislodge curls of coiled springs

condemn our shared memories
to the grave.

## Rum, Sodomy and the Lash

I peel the strip of cellophane
to re-release the Pogues
into a sea-swept pub
inside a wind-swept town
where a voice
like heels on gravel
carved my path

when lipstick and eyeliner opened
doors and Carlsberg Specials,
shillings filled glasses
and shoulders swayed
as hands tapped beer mats
on tidal tables

and full to the brim
sea whispers lassoed our shoes
sinking in sand.

A time when friendship
outlived passion and
passion was a long player
a place last orders
were never called.

## Carrigart

We drove to the furthest point
the Atlantic coast
it took us less time than expected.

They spoke a foreign language
there, though we recognised
a word like slán
from our classroom days.

We longed for turf
for ashes in the hearth
as we sipped lager shandies
around a two-bar fire

while in mute half-light
men, characters in their own play,
parked their bones on stools
wiped froth from their
wrinkled kisses.

We watched them from our chairs
our voices hushed
fearful we might put an end
to their lives

not that we sought it for ourselves
we were merely voyeurs
tigresses
stalking through.

## Liquid cliffs

listen
for my step
recall
my imprint
in fuchsia hedge

a seagull's call
in letraset
relieves me
of my skin.

## Glen Strand

Colour me green
sweep me into deep water

where no moss impedes
the movement of my limbs

nor pinched stone blisters
the underbelly of my blanket.

Colour me green
and I will withstand

unfriendly banter
caustic erosions

crumbling only
where it does not show.

## The Shark and the Albatross

A swimmer
in the endless under blue
stalks a victim
and like his tiger's namesake
is secure in his territory
a voracious hunter
ominous and silent
looming.


A flyer in the over endless blue
this chick's tight schedule
has too short a runway
for its maiden flight
and fluttering ungainly
he touches down on a wet strip
squawking unbalanced
off course.


The school tightens the circle
and the holy sea foams
but no whistle blows
and pearly white teeth
crunch down on young bones
exult on broken wings.

I feel her


slipping
        through my fingers
like wind through
        a dream-catcher's web

appearing over
        sand dunes
her feet barely touching
        the ground

dirndl skirt billowing
        head full of treasure
she hunts for
        square stones

or indian feathers
        elusive as a
red admiral caught
        in an offshore wind.

You remind me

of a line in a poem
I can't quite recall

of fir trees in sand
sand dunes in May

of even-tempered butterscotch
names slip, slip-sliding away

of flames in flamenco dresses
scorch marks in the dance

and the final heel-toe
together-step-hop.

# Last tango in Venice

An Argentine mist rises
over Piazza San Marco
embraces a public
drawing room lined
with arcane arches
and stirring tandas.
A dancer strides out
under the moon lamps
leads a man,
spreading into autumn,
from a grand café.
A raven-haired willow
in short, red skirt
keeps her reluctant
partner close
walks a rhythmic pulse
ankles and knees brush
one leg passes the other
toe of her stiletto drawing
patterns on the tiles.
Eyes almost touching lips
she tugs, pushes
turns, dips, hesitates
elongates in slow
measured moves
keeping him close,
chest-to-chest
a visual heart-to-heartbeat.

## Attending the opera in Prague

I walk on squares of toffee
block against Czech block
shade against ground
breaking shade
taste the sticky days of '89.

Gentiles now fill Jewish quarters
Kafka balances on headless
shoulders and a socialist museum
caresses the velvet revolution.

The sea-curtain falls
like a gossamer wave
a buoyancy aid for
water nymphs
for Rusalka who sings
for love on terra firma
barters with her voice

while two seats over
golden tones of violins
catch in the throat
of a woman smiling
behind an anxious mask.

In praise of Manuel Gonzalez
Barcelona 2005


Wrapped
in mute black coats
three hundred breaths
crystallise under
Santa Marie del Pi
as Gothic buttresses
arch their backs
and he dances
chilled fingers on
strings of silver
and bronze
changes tempo
to melt lovers
in their lairs
tears on the tongue
stones in iced effigies.

I remove my gloves
feel the blood flow.

## Visiting the Dostoyevskys

A second floor apartment
made wondrous by its tenants:

the floor he paced
she swept

seven windows he witnessed
she wiped

their children's notes
she slipped beneath his door

and on her desk
a splinter from the brothers

on his a clock
stopped

at the hour of his death.

## All our Saturdays

In the white of a winter's day
a line of sheets stand firm
each one a safety curtain

primed to rise majestically
silencing sweet
rustlings among the

flicks and crackles
of the latest screen buster.
She flips her seat

ready to boo the baddy
swoon at the bri nylon guy
until fumblers in the

back row button up
and she buys
a single in the chippy.

My bucket list

If an eminent surgeon
told me I had six
months to live
I'd go in search
of a polar bear.
Making a pact with
the devil's mother and
leaving nothing to chance
I'd work my passage
on a liner bound for Alaska.
Abandoning ship
I'd hijack a sleigh
and ten huskies
race against time
pick-pockets
icy winds
until I find him
in the whiteness
of the desert and
I'd say to the thief
on my shoulder
take a picture
take a picture of
the devil's mother
the polar bear and me.

## Wishing Stone

A stone face leans
on a granite pillow
ear cocked to
expectant eggstone
crusted in myth
and silence
as he stands
by the open door
waits to turn
the wishing tide
curse the day
she was born.

## Insomnia

I perch on a precipice
like an eagle I perch
talons fused in arthritic grip
as I count geese in the feathers
of my pillow, breathe deep
in the rise and fall
of a wide-awake duvet
while you hide behind
green fluorescent figures
that blind the room
with incurable time.
I fight you on the beaches
eager for early submission
throw countless towels
into the ring and still
you are the last one standing
and I curse you
in the groan of the stairs
in the fuse box
in the hum of the dancing fridge
that invites me to join the party
with TV and DVD
and I know that judgment day
is coming when a clear conscience
sleeps with eyes wide shut.

# Keeping the spirit level

It's all about keeping
the spirit level
bubble in view
as it travels
at the slightest
inclination through
the alcohol tube
low viscosity
and a yellow hue.

Below the plane
you are lost
gasping for air -
above
and a rush
soars you high
as a kite on a string
susceptible
to a drop in pressure
or a sharp scissors.

**Blue Mountain**

## The Blue Mountain

A spit of snow lies on Croghan's face
jilted after the cold snap
that left parishes standing
like Miss Havisham in her mottled gown.

It needs snow to move snow, they say
so in expectation I watch
for a battleship sky
to snag itself on the blue peak
scarred by chainsaw
damaged forests, promises
while below me
the river Bann cuts
through reeds and green willow
as I trace the line of its curve,
rush of shallows
silence of its deep
imagine how it feels to walk
over mud-raked copper fields
and slip into the naked water
step by step.

Back on the road again
I stand at an altered hedgerow
swollen with marigold gloves
broken bottles, crushed vows
gather them up for the tip.

## Sorcery in Caheraderry

The home grows from a ring fort
through the clay of Caheraderry
as we fish lines of syllables
from grey Liscannor stone.

Across a marshy field, flag irises
shine through this greener grass
oversee the lift and return
of two coffin stools

legs turned vermicular and
splayed to take the load -
appanages of dignity that lightly
held a master's weight a month ago.

And like the sorcerer's apprentice
we witness the breaking of a spell
that turns coffin stools back
into occasional tables.

## The final battle

I am tired of the battle
with dragons and dragoons
of laying out my armour
at each sunrise and sunset.


Did Cúchulainn fear the next
smear of blood on his axe
Lir's silver chained swans
the next sip of green water.


When did breathing
become so important.

## Deirdre and Naoise

If only I'd listened
censured our passion
the moment of conception
instead we fled offshore
like Deirdre and Naoise
with Cathbadh's words
snapping at our heels.

For a while we were
happy in our misery
fearful that tomorrow
would strip the flesh
from our bones and

when that day came
and words made flesh
you leapt like Deirdre
from her chariot
sorrowed in your distress.

It is said
on the fated lovers' graves
two trees entwine –
other endings are predictable
like a straight line.

## Lost snakes of Ireland

You wake from the peace
of my oak mantle
cloaked in kiln-fired grey
your shovel chin, wry smile
one with the poet's flame.

Lore-master of the snake
keeper of a people
in spirit with the earth
there is healing in your robes
and wisdom seeded in the roots
of the oak-green groves.

I weep for those roots ripped
from your safekeeping
your serpent staff fractured
by armies of saints clad
in sackcloth and axes.

May you once more cut mistletoe
with a golden knife, sacrifice
two white bulls in a grove of oak
and, without paying the taxman's fine,
may your soul pass into mine.

## Ripped

I found her
between hedges
stiff with rage
bits of flesh and bone
heard her deep
within me
still
but breathing
cold
but ticking
smelt the stench.

I wasn't looking
for adventure
when I stumbled
and fell
but they thought
it was me
I found her
bits of flesh and bone.

I find you crying in the corner

for your god-forsaken life
and who would blame you.

You have it all you tell me
and I know that's untrue

as I watch you flaunting
what I've mislaid

and tomorrow
if the devil's on the high road

I will take my 'all'
stretch my legs

take a stroll on the
other side of intimacy.

## The fall of Jericho

A trumpet blows
throws bricks
like confetti
overhead.
It took seven days
for their walls
to tumble and
a shout
so clamorous
as to render
the fall of Jericho.

First draft

You glare at me
from the page

a black spot
on a white lung

breathless
like a fly

marinated
in silence

a leaf pressed
between new sheets

a zeal of letters
climbing out
of a birthing pool.

## Washing the dirty linen

On her landing a cupboard
of white linen presses against
planed wooden bars
separated by misgivings.
She did not mean to lie
for like wearing fancy dress
her aim was to deceive

and on dislocated days
she believed the bearers of truth
that lay on her tongue
like wet clay on a gated grave.
It was simply an error of judgement –
a truth held in a sheep-skinned hand
cleared a field stonier than her track.

Now on washing day her iron cools
towels dissemble, bedspreads hole
her bleached hands mislead
the cloudy waters and unlike the stork
her blue phoenix flies on one wing
nestles its egg in a bed of broken twigs.

Winds of change

Walking through
a postcard of Vermont

I stumble on an orchestra
of painted deckchairs

tuning their instruments
in the wind

feet testing the water
clouds like white towels

draped over each arm
waiting for the tide to turn.

## The shower

Barefoot
in the flow
drenched
by a forest
of pine
his nakedness
naked
love-strung
his arms flung
into spray
like wings
of a swan
rising from
Lough Dan.

## Mixed Media in Botanic Gardens

I stand naked in a marble jungle
covered by copper wire and bronze
flesh stained with new rain

                           ceramic curves

          surprises in the grass.

My mind sings
imprinted on paper clay
emptied by eggshells

                          forgotten shells

          chickenwire

reclothed in crystal and alabaster.

## Streets of fear

The street is liquid with intrigue
        as I Sherlock underground
side-step yellow streams
        and living graveyards
of the underpass

where your shadow stalks
        a line of parked cars
clings to their bodies
        like 2-in-1 oil
pursuing me and my lover.

A close shave

The sun has left the front
and a sea breeze marshals
a militia of fine hairs on my arms.

I take my skin around the back
to surrender to the peace of sun
and long, long view

when a gunshot startles
a battalion
shakes out black shrapnel
from the trees
to pepper the sky.

Caught in the silence
of the cease-fire
my fear retreats to the rookery
bears no grudge
accepts the close shave.

## Couplets to friendship

I do not know how it comes
nor can count the ways

but come it does
as light off a full moon's face

in a bottle stranded on a beach
or letters tangled in a net

on a Wexford train
or any train

in the 'Hi' of a mobile text
that you least expect

walking in when the whole
world walks out

filling days as copiously
as days fill years.

## The table

A woman filled with rememberings
laid her table out.

She put brown bread and jam there
the dent in a white mudguard of a red
tricycle, a six berth caravan filled with
egg-timer sand.

She put there a bottle-green uniform
the measles and fluffy-pink calamine lotion
a rocking cot in baby blue.

On that table she put ankle socks
swinging on an occasional table
and a sometimes hard-back Pinocchio.

She laid her broken finger there
a late 62 bus and the night the conductor
closed the doors on quick-eyed boys.

Her first and last suspender belt
a ladder in her stocking
she put there, and reaching over

she placed twenty-one
years on that table
the sound of London's underground

the flicker of fear in city shadows
the cry of the lonesome
and finally on that table

the woman put her blue and white
wedding dress wrapped
in a tarnished gold ring.

And as the table began to wobble
she wedged under the leg
a folded envelope with the words

freedom is never free.

## Notes

Page 1: Aphrodisia. Reference to Cleopatra's show-stopping entry by barge into Tarsus to cultivate Mark Antony's support.

Page 2: Lost in Laurence's Arabia. Reference to the battle to conquer the port of Aqaba as depicted in the film *Lawrence of Arabia.*

Page 12: I plant a yew. Lanceolate is a lance shaped leaf.
Straight-tusked elephant (Pleistocene) was found at Lehringen, Germany, with the remains of a yew spear between its ribs.

Page 13: Crossing the bog of Alan. A well-preserved Iron Age body was found in an Irish bog in June 2003. The find is on display in the National Museum of Ireland in Dublin.

Page 14: Ladies in Lavender. *Ladies in Lavender* is a 2004 British film.

Page 17: The dreaming time.  Reference to Bruce Chatwin's novel *The Songlines*.

Page 22: Reading Akhmatova. Anna Akhmatova is a distinguished Russian poet. The 'breathing space' refers to a period of reprieve during Stalin's reign.

Page 28: Rum, Sodomy and the Lash. Title of album by The Pogues (band).

Page 33: I feel her. A dirndl skirt is a full skirt with gathered waistband.

Page 35: Last tango in Venice. A tanda is a turn of dancing in a milonga and, by association, a set of pieces of music.

Page 36: Attending the opera in Prague. *Rusalka* is an opera based on the Little Mermaid story.

Page 38: Visiting the Dostoyevskys. The brothers refers to Dostoyevsky's novel *The Brothers Karamazov*.

Page 41: Wishing Stone. Inspired by sculpture by Séighean Ó'Draoi.

Page 46: The Blue Mountain. Miss Havisham is a character in *Great Expectations* by Charles Dickens who was jilted on her wedding day.

Page 47: Sorcery in Caheraderry. Appanages are hereditary rights that belong to one by custom.
The Sorcerer's Apprentice is a poem by Goethe (1797) popularized by the film *Fantasia*.

Page 48: The final battle. Cúchulainn is an Irish mythological warrior.
*The Children of Lir* is an Irish legend about children turned into swans for 900 years.

Page 49: Deirdre and Naoise. The title refers to the ill-fated lovers in Irish mythology.

Page 50: Lost snakes of Ireland. Some scholars contend that the snake was originally a symbol for Irish druids.

Page 51: Ripped. Reference to a victim of the Yorkshire Ripper found by a passer-by.